Bb CLARINET

CONCERT FAVORITES

Volume 1

Band Arrangements Correlated with
Essential Elements Band Method Book 1

ISBN 978-0-634-05202-6

7777 W. BLUEMOUND RD. P.O. BOX 13819 MILWAUKEE, WI 53213

00860122

LET'S ROCK!

Bb CLARINET

MICHAEL SWEENEY (ASCAP)

00860122

MAJESTIC MARCH

B♭ CLARINET

By PAUL LAVENDER

MICKEY MOUSE MARCH
(From Walt Disney's "THE MICKEY MOUSE CLUB")

Bb CLARINET

Words and Music by JIMMIE DODD
Arranged by MICHAEL SWEENEY

00860122

POWER ROCK
(We Will Rock You • Another One Bites The Dust)

Bb CLARINET

Arranged by MICHAEL SWEENEY

00860122

WHEN THE SAINTS GO MARCHING IN

Words by KATHERINE E. PURVIS
Music by JAMES M. BLACK
Arranged by JOHN HIGGINS

B♭ CLARINET

FARANDOLE
(From "L'Arlésienne")

Bb CLARINET

GEORGES BIZET
Arranged by MICHAEL SWEENEY (ASCAP)

00860122

JUS' PLAIN BLUES

B♭ CLARINET

MICHAEL SWEENEY (ASCAP)

MY HEART WILL GO ON
(Love Theme From 'Titanic')

Music by JAMES HORNER
Lyric by WILL JENNINGS
Arranged by PAUL LAVENDER

B♭ CLARINET

From THE MUPPET MOVIE

THE RAINBOW CONNECTION

Words and Music by PAUL WILLIAMS
and KENNITH L. ASCHER
Arranged by PAUL LAVENDER

B♭ CLARINET

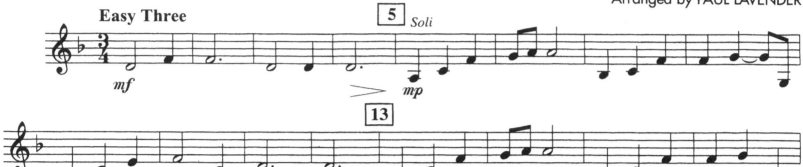

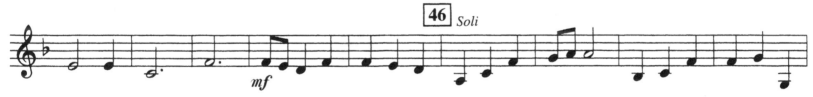

00860122

SUPERCALIFRAGILISTICEXPIALIDOCIOUS

Words and Music by
RICHARD M. SHERMAN and ROBERT B. SHERMAN
Arranged by MICHAEL SWEENEY

B♭ Clarinet

00860122

(From "THE SOUND OF MUSIC")
DO-RE-MI

Bb CLARINET

Lyrics by OSCAR HAMMERSTEIN II
Music by RICHARD RODGERS
Arranged by PAUL LAVENDER

00860122

DRUMS OF CORONA

Bb CLARINET

MICHAEL SWEENEY (ASCAP)

LAREDO
(Concert March)

Bb CLARINET

JOHN HIGGINS

00860122

14

POMP AND CIRCUMSTANCE
March No. 1

B♭ CLARINET

By EDWARD ELGAR
Arranged by MICHAEL SWEENEY

00860122

STRATFORD MARCH

B♭ CLARINET

JOHN HIGGINS (ASCAP)